Plan, Prepare, COOK

A Tasty Breakfast

Rita Storey

A⁺
Smart Apple Media

Contents

Published by Smart Apple Media,
an imprint of Black Rabbit Books
P.O. Box 3263, Mankato, Minnesota 56002
www.blackrabbitbooks.com

U.S. publication copyright © 2015 Smart Apple
Media. International copyright reserved in all
countries. No part of this book may be reproduced
in any form without written permission from the
publisher.

Printed in the United States by Worzalla,
Stevens Point, Wisconsin.
PO1655
4-2014

Published by arrangement with the
Watts Publishing Group LTD, London.

Library of Congress Cataloging-in-Publication Data
Storey, Rita.
 A tasty breakfast / Rita Storey.
    pages cm. -- (Plan, prepare, cook)
 Includes index.
 Audience: Grade 4 to 6.
 ISBN 978-1-59920-953-1
 1. Breakfasts--Juvenile literature. I. Title.
 TX733.S76 2015
 641.5'2--dc23
                                    2013034772

Picture credits
All photographs Tudor Photography, Banbury
unless otherwise stated. Shutterstock p5;
Wishlistimages.co.uk p4

Cover images Tudor Photography
All photos posed by models. Thanks to Serena
Clayton, Adam Hedley, and Emma Whitehouse.

Free activity sheets are available for pages marked with ⬇. Request them at info@blackrabbitbooks.com. Find out more on page 32.

Words in **bold** are in the glossary on page 30.

Before You Start

These simple rules will make sure you stay safe when you cook:

- Wash your hands before and after preparing food.
- Ask an adult to help when the recipe uses the oven or stovetop.
- If you have long hair, clip or tie it back.
- Dry your hands before you plug in or unplug any electrical appliances.
- Wear an apron or an old shirt.
- Wash up as you go along.
- Be extra careful with sharp knives.
- Ask an adult to help with the blender/food processor.
- Ask an adult to help you measure the ingredients.

Look for this useful guide to each recipe.

How long each recipe takes to make.

How difficult each recipe is to make.

Whether the recipe needs to be cooked.

All about Breakfast

What you eat and drink is called your **diet**. To eat a **balanced diet**, try not to have the same foods every day. There are so many tasty foods and drinks to choose from at breakfast time—why stick to the same things every day?

The Human Machine

The human body is a machine that needs **energy** to work. Energy is released from the food we eat and used by our bodies.

Meat, Fish, Chicken, Eggs, and Beans

These foods contain **protein**. Eggs are often eaten at breakfast time.

Fruit and Vegetables

You should eat at least five portions of fruit and vegetables every day. They should make up about a third of what you eat. Frozen, canned, and dried fruits and vegetables all count. Try to eat lots of different types.

• A glass of fruit juice counts as one portion, so try to have one at breakfast time.

Make a Good Start

Eating a good breakfast will give you the energy to concentrate throughout the morning. If you do not have breakfast, you may feel tired and grumpy until you can eat at lunchtime.

Exercise

When you **exercise,** you use up the energy from the food you have eaten.

To be healthy, you need to eat enough food but not too much. If you eat more food than your body needs, it is turned into **fat**. If you do this all the time, you keep getting fatter.

Playing a sport, walking, riding your bike, or dancing are all good ways to exercise.

Other people may enjoy exercising with you!

Starchy Foods

You should eat **starchy** foods every day—they should make up about a third of what you eat. A portion of bread or cereal at breakfast time is a good start to the day.

- Choose **whole grain** or **whole wheat** varieties.

A Healthy Body

To stay healthy, your body needs some things found in food and drinks. **Vitamins** and **minerals** help to keep you from getting sick. You also need them for your body to grow and work properly. Different foods contain different vitamins and minerals. To make sure you get all the vitamins and minerals you need, eat plenty of fruit and vegetables as well as a range of other foods. **Fiber** is needed to help your body **digest** the food you eat.

Milk and Yogurt

Milk and all types of yogurt are a good choice to put on cereals at breakfast time.

- Use **2%** milk as it has less fat.

- Look at the labels on yogurt, and choose the ones lowest in sugar and fat.

Shopping and Planning

Planning, preparing, and cooking great-tasting food for yourself, friends, and family is great fun, and you get to eat well too!

Think of all the things you would like to make for breakfast in the next week. Look through this book for some new ideas for breakfast recipes. Make a shopping list of the things you need.

Make a shopping list of the things you need to make a tasty breakfast every day for a week.

Go Shopping

If you go shopping for food, look at the food labels. Some foods are very good for you. Foods that are high in salt, sugar, or fat are bad for you if you eat them too often.

- Choose whole grain or whole wheat bread and breakfast cereals. They have lots of vitamins, minerals, and fiber (see page 5). They also have lots of flavor.

• Look for low-salt, low-sugar, and low-fat foods (particularly if the fat is **saturated fat**) on food labels.

Plan Ahead

Breakfast time can be a rush, so prepare things in advance if you can. Pancake **batter**, fruit salad, and smoothie drinks can all be made the night before you need them and kept in the fridge. Fruit bars (see pages 16-17) will keep for a few days in a plastic container.

When you wake up you will know that you can make a delicious breakfast quickly.

Sugar, Fat, and Processed Foods

Foods from this group should only be eaten occasionally.
• Avoid white bread and white sugar.
• Look for cereals that do not have added sugar.
• Sausages and bacon are often eaten for breakfast. They have a lot of fat in them. Just have them every now and again as a treat.
• Use only a small amount of butter or oil in cooking.

Make sure you drink enough water.

Water

You need water for your body to perform well. You get some water from the foods you eat. You should drink six to eight glasses of water a day—more in hot weather.

Fruit Smoothie

Not all healthy breakfasts are cooked. This simple fruit smoothie drink has lots of good things in it to give you energy in the morning.

You Will Need

- measuring cup
- blender (or food processor)
- measuring spoons
- drinking glass
- drinking straw

Ingredients

- 1 ripe banana
- some strawberries or raspberries
- 2 cups (425 ml) milk
- 4 tablespoons Greek yogurt

This will make enough for two large glasses.

If You Prefer

Use banana or strawberry yogurt instead of Greek yogurt.

Add a teaspoon of honey to unsweetened yogurt.

1

- Peel the banana.
- Put the banana and any other fruits you are using in the blender.

2

- Measure the milk with the measuring cup.
- Pour the milk into the blender.

- Put 4 tablespoons of Greek yogurt in the blender.

- Put the lid on the blender. Turn the blender on.

- Blend everything together until there are no lumps.

- Pour the mixture into a glass and enjoy a healthy and delicious breakfast drink.

Mmm!

Handy Hint
This drink will keep for two days in a screw-top bottle in the fridge.

10 minutes

Very easy

No cooking

Fruit Salad

This colorful fruit salad is a fresh and tasty way to start the day.

You Will Need
- paper towel
- sharp knife
- cutting board
- teaspoon
- peeler
- mixing bowl
- mixing spoon
- bowl and spoon

Ingredients

- selection of different colored fruits: oranges, bananas, strawberries, kiwi fruit, blueberries, seedless grapes (about ½ cup [90 g.] per person)
- teaspoon of lemon juice
- ½ cup (125 ml) unsweetened fruit juice

Handy Hint

Different colored fruits and vegetables contain a variety of vitamins and minerals (see page 5).

Before You Start

- Wash the fruit and pat it dry on a paper towel.

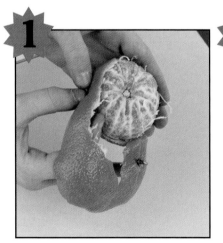

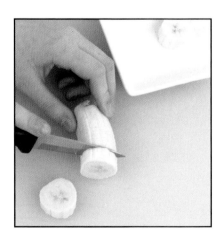

Oranges
- Take off the peel.

- Divide into segments.

Bananas
- Peel and slice. Toss in the lemon juice to keep the slices from turning brown.

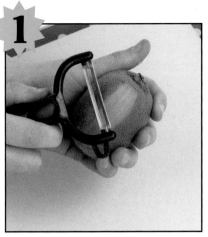

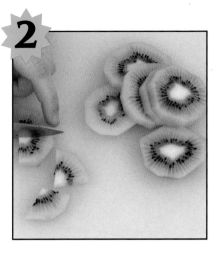

Strawberries
- Take off the leaves and stems. Cut in half.

Kiwi Fruit
- Using the peeler, take off the peel.

- Cut into slices. Cut the slices in half, and then in half again.

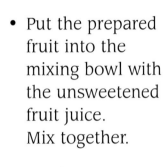

- Put the prepared fruit into the mixing bowl with the unsweetened fruit juice. Mix together.

Grapes
Cut in half.

Beautiful!

Serve in a plain bowl to show off all the bright rainbow colors.

15 minutes

Medium

No cooking

Berry Cereal

A bowl of cereal is a quick and easy breakfast. To make it into a really healthy meal, add a handful of fresh berries.

You Will Need

- strainer
- paper towel
- cutting board
- small sharp knife
- cereal bowl
- spoon

Ingredients

- handful of berries such as strawberries, raspberries, blackberries, or blueberries
- portion of cereal
- 2% milk

Choosing a Breakfast Cereal
Look at the ingredients list on the box of breakfast cereal. If possible, use a breakfast cereal that does not have any added sugar. The best kind of cereal is whole grain or whole wheat with nothing else added. If necessary, you can sweeten it yourself with a small amount of sugar or honey.

1

- Put the berries in the strainer and rinse in cold water.

2

- Pat them dry with a paper towel.

- Cut large fruits into smaller pieces.

- Pour the cereal into a bowl.

- Pour on the milk.

- Sprinkle on the berries.

Handy Hint

You can use other fruits if you prefer. See pages 10 and 11 for how to prepare them.

Wow!

5 minutes

Very easy

No cooking

Yogurt Mix-up

This messy, crunchy breakfast is full of healthy things to get your day off to a good start. Try making it with your favorite breakfast cereal.

Ingredients

- 1 small banana
- 2½ tablespoons Greek yogurt
- a heaped tablespoon of bran flakes or cornflakes
- honey

You Will Need

- kitchen knife
- mixing bowl
- mixing spoon
- cereal bowl
- spoon

If You Prefer

You can use any type of yogurt or cottage cheese in this recipe. Try a few different combinations. Other fruits such as chunks of apple and apricots are also very good. Only use honey if the yogurt is unsweetened.

Yogurt

Yogurt contains **calcium** which helps to build strong bones and teeth. It also contains protein, vitamins, and minerals. Low-fat yogurt contains all these things but has less fat. Some yogurt has a lot of sugar added to it.

1

- Peel the banana.
- Slice it and put the slices into the mixing bowl.

2

- Put the yogurt into the mixing bowl.

3

- Add the cereal.
- Mix everything together gently so that the flakes of cereal do not get too broken up.

- Serve in a cereal bowl with a drizzle of honey.

Yummmmm

5 minutes

Very easy

No cooking

Chewy Fruit Bar

If there really is no time for breakfast, try one of these bars instead. They are packed full of fruity energy.

You Will Need

- food processor (or blender)
- small saucepan
- wooden spoon
- non-stick baking sheet
- knife
- small strainer

Ingredients

- ¾ cup (115 g.) trail mix (a mixture of dried fruits and nuts)
- ½ cup (30 g.) mini marshmallows
- 1 tablespoon of water
- 1 teaspoon powdered sugar

Handy Hint

Sugar is bad for your teeth. If you have any foods that contain sugar at breakfast time, remember to brush your teeth afterwards.

1

- Pour the trail mix into the food processor.

2

- Blend until there are no big lumps.

3

- Put the marshmallows and water into a small saucepan. Put the pan on the burner on low heat.

- Stir with the wooden spoon until the marshmallows have melted.

- Add the blended trail mix and stir until well mixed.

- Spoon the mixture onto the baking sheet.
- Remember to turn the burner off.

- Press the mixture down with the knife. Put in the fridge.
- When set, cut into squares.

- Sift the powdered sugar over the fruit bars.

Yummy!

| 1 hour |
| Easy |
| Cooked |

Cheesy Eggs

Ingredients

- 2 eggs
- 3 tablespoons grated cheese (see page 29)
- 1 slice whole grain bread, muffin, or bagel, toasted
- 2 tablespoons butter

Eggs are a good, healthy breakfast choice. There are lots of different ways to cook them for breakfast.

You Will Need

- small mixing bowl
- fork
- tablespoon
- knife
- small non-stick saucepan
- wooden spoon
- plate

Bread

Bread is made from wheat. It is a starchy food, like pasta, potatoes, and rice. Bread has vitamins, minerals, and fiber in it (see page 5). Most types of white bread have less fiber than whole grain bread.

1

- Crack the eggs into the mixing bowl (see page 28).
- Whisk the eggs with the fork until the white and the yolk are all mixed together.

2

- Stir in the grated cheese with a spoon.

- Spread the bagel with half the butter.
- Turn on the burner. Put the pan on the burner on low heat.

- Melt the other half of the butter in the saucepan on the burner.

- Pour the egg and cheese mixture into the saucepan.

- Stir the mixture with the wooden spoon until it is cooked. You will see the color of the mixture change as you stir it.
- Remember to turn the burner off.

- Put the buttered bagel on the plate. Spoon the cheesy eggs onto it. Add a sprinkle of grated cheese.

Cheesylicious!

| 10 minutes |
| Medium |
| Cooked |

"Just Right" Oatmeal

The three bears in the "Goldilocks" story knew all about eating a good breakfast. A bowl of oatmeal is a great way to start the day. Oats are cheap to buy and easy to cook.

Ingredients

- ½ cup (60 g.) rolled oats
- 1 cup (240 ml) 2% milk
- handful of dried cranberries
- drizzle of maple syrup or honey

Oats

Oats are a starchy food (see page 5). They are used up slowly in your body so they make you feel full for a long time. They also contain lots of fiber. Buy "rolled oats" rather than "instant oats." Oats should be the only ingredient on the label!

You Will Need

- measuring cups
- small non-stick saucepan
- wooden spoon
- cereal bowl and spoon

1

- Put the oats into the saucepan and add the milk.
- Turn the burner on to medium heat.

2

- Stir the oatmeal with the wooden spoon.
- When the oatmeal starts to bubble, turn the heat down to low and keep stirring for 2 minutes.
- Remember to turn the burner off.

- Spoon the oatmeal mixture into a cereal bowl.
- Top with the dried cranberries.

- Add a drizzle of maple syrup or honey.

Handy Hint

When you have put the cooked oatmeal into the bowl, fill the dirty saucepan with water to make it easier to wash up.

Scrumptious

5 minutes

Easy

Cooked

Muesli Magic

Muesli is a breakfast cereal made from rolled oats mixed with nuts, seeds, and dried fruits. You can eat it with milk or use this recipe to turn it into something really special to impress your family and friends.

Ingredients

- ⅓ cup (30 g.) rolled oats
- ¼ cup (30 g.) dried fruits (raisins, apricots, dried apple chunks, dried cranberries) and ¼ cup (30 g.) chopped nuts
- 2 tablespoons plain thick, Greek, or vanilla yogurt
- 1 tablespoon of fruit sauce
- ½ cup (60 g.) raspberries
- honey

Muesli

You can buy muesli ready-mixed in stores. Look on the box for a muesli that has no added sugar and salt. Many prepared cereals contain a lot of sugar and salt.

1

- Mix the oats, fruits, and nuts in a bowl.

2

- In another bowl, mix the fruit sauce with 1 tablespoon of yogurt.

- Put 1 tablespoon of plain yogurt in the bottom of the glass.
- Sprinkle a layer of muesli on top of the yogurt.
- Add a layer of raspberries.

4

- Add a layer of the yogurt and fruit sauce mixture.
- Finish with a layer of muesli and a drizzle of honey.

Mmmmm

10 minutes

Easy

No cooking

23

Fruit Pancakes

Pancakes are made from a mixture of milk, flour, and eggs, called batter. Make a stack and fill with your favorite fruits.

You Will Need

- strainer
- mixing bowl
- measuring spoons
- fork
- measuring cups
- whisk
- frying pan
- spatula
- plate

Ingredients

- 1 cup (115 g.) all-purpose flour
- 3 teaspoons baking powder
- pinch of salt
- 1 tablespoon sugar
- 1 egg
- ¾ cup (175 ml) milk
- 2 tablespoons oil
- a few tablespoons of prepared fruit
- whipped cream or yogurt
- chopped nuts
- honey or maple syrup

This will make 12 pancakes.

Other Fillings

- applesauce and a sprinkle of cinnamon
- cherry pie filling and a spoonful of ice cream

1
- Sift the flour, baking powder, and salt into the mixing bowl.
- Add the sugar.

2
- Crack the egg into the measuring cup (see page 28). Whisk it up with a fork.

3
- Add the egg to the dry ingredients in the mixing bowl.
- Add the milk.

- Whisk it all together.
- Put half a teaspoon of oil into a frying pan. Heat the frying pan over medium heat.

- Drop in a tablespoon of batter.
- Cook for about a minute until bubbles appear on the surface.

- Turn the pancake over with the spatula. Cook the other side for about a minute.

- Place the pancake on a plate and keep warm.
- Make more pancakes until all the mixture is used.
- Stack the pancakes, putting fruit and whipped cream or yogurt between them.
- Top with chopped nuts and honey or maple syrup.
- Remember to turn the burner off when the cooking is finished.

Perfect

| 30 minutes |
| Tricky! |
| Cooked |

Eggs and Toast

The combination of boiled egg and crunchy whole wheat toast fingers makes a perfect breakfast. The egg and toast are easy to cook and good for you, too.

Ingredients

- 1 egg
- 1 slice whole wheat bread, toasted
- 2 tablespoons butter

You Will Need

- small saucepan
- egg timer
- spoon
- egg cup
- small plate
- knife

Eggs
Eggs are a good source of protein, and contain vitamins and minerals.
Free range eggs are from hens that are allowed to run around in the open air.
Barn eggs are from hens that are kept in big barns.

1

- Turn the burner on high.
- Put the egg into the saucepan and cover it with cold water.
  Put it on the burner.

2

- When the water starts to **boil** (see page 29), turn the egg timer over.
  If you do not have an egg timer, time three minutes on a clock.
- When all the sand has gone to the bottom of the timer, lift the egg out of the pan with a spoon.

3

- Put the egg into the egg cup.
- Remember to turn the burner off.
- Cut the top off the egg with the spoon, or peel off the egg shell. Be careful! It will be hot.

4

- Butter the toast.

5

- Cut it into strips.

6

- Dip the strips into the egg.

Love It!

10 minutes

Easy

Cooked

How To!

Crack Open an Egg

1
- Tap the egg gently on the side of a bowl so that it cracks.

2
- Put your thumbs on either side of the crack.

3
- Hold the egg over the bowl and gently pull the shell apart.

Use a Strainer

1

You can sift flour and powdered sugar to get rid of any lumps.
- Place the strainer on top of a bowl.
- Put the measured ingredient (usually flour or powdered sugar) into the strainer.
- Lift the strainer up above the bowl and gently tap it against the palm of your hand. The sifted flour or sugar will fall into the bowl. Any lumps of flour or sugar can be gently pushed through the strainer with a spoon.

Grate

1

- Hold the top of the grater to keep it from slipping.

2

- Press food against the blades and push down.

- A food grater has lots of sharp blades that can turn food into strips.
- A box grater has different-sized blades for different foods.
- Cheese and carrots are best grated on the largest blades.
- The smallest blades are for grating the rind off oranges and lemons.

Whisk

To whisk means to stir something quickly to mix everything together. Whisking adds air to a mixture to make it lighter.

- A whisk is a kitchen utensil designed for whisking liquids.

- This egg is being whisked with a fork.

Know When Water is Boiling

- Cold water does not have any bubbles.
- As the water heats up, small bubbles rise to the surface. The water is **simmering**.

- As the water gets hotter the bubbles get larger and pop as they rise to the surface. The water is now boiling.

Glossary

balanced diet A diet that contains all the foods necessary to grow and stay healthy.

batter A mixture of flour, egg, and milk, used for making pancakes and muffins, or to coat food before it is fried.

boiling The point at which water (or another liquid) reaches a heat when it bubbles and turns into steam.

calcium A mineral that the body needs to develop healthy bones and teeth. Calcium is found in foods such as milk, yogurt, and cheese.

diet The things that you eat and drink.

digest To break down food inside the body so that it can be converted into energy.

energy A type of power that can be used. Food is changed to energy in your body.

exercise Physical activity that uses up calories and improves fitness.

fat A greasy substance found in food. Fats are divided into two types: **saturated fats** are found in cream, cheese, butter, fatty meat, and chocolate; **unsaturated fats** are found in avocados, nuts, vegetable oils, and olive oils. Unsaturated fats are healthier than saturated fats.

fiber The part of a fruit or vegetable that cannot be digested. Fiber helps the digestion of other food.

mineral A substance such as iron and calcium that the body needs to function properly. Minerals are found in foods.

processed food Any food product that has been changed in some way. Cooking, freezing, drying, canning, and preserving are all methods of processing food. Processed foods may contain colorings, flavorings, and other additives and preservatives.

protein A substance found in some foods. It is needed by the body to grow and develop properly. Meat, eggs, milk, and some types of beans contain protein.

simmering To bring a liquid almost to a boil. A simmering liquid has small bubbles that rise to the surface.

starchy A food containing starch. Starchy foods make up one of the food groups. They include bread, cereals, rice, pasta, and potatoes.

vitamin One of the substances that are essential in very small amounts in the body for normal growth and activity.

whole grain A cereal such as wheat, barley, or oats that has not had the outer layer taken off.

whole wheat The entire grain of wheat including the outer layer (bran).

Equipment

non-stick baking sheet

little strainer

big strainer

cutting board

measuring cup

spatula

grater

mixing bowl

mixing spoon

whisk

tablespoon

teaspoon

non-stick saucepan

small sharp knife

knife

frying pan

egg timer

wooden spoons

You will also need:
dish towel
oven mitt
measuring cups
measuring spoons

paper towels

blender

food processor

Index

Activity Sheets

Request these free activity sheets at: info@blackrabbitbooks.com.

Pages 4–5 All about Breakfast

Plan your breakfasts for the week ahead on this handy food chart. Fill in the shopping list so you know what you need to buy.

Pages 6–7 All about Breakfast

What do your friends eat for breakfast? Fill in this food survey to find out what is the most popular breakfast.

Page 31 Equipment

Download a colorful poster of all the equipment used in the *"Plan, Prepare, Cook"* books.